D1101231

KENT GAVIN frps

My Royal Appointments

First published in May 2012

All rights reserved. No part of this publication may be reproduced, stored
in a retrieval system, or transmitted, in any form by any means, electronic,
mechanical, photocopying, recording or otherwise, without prior
permission of the publisher.

© Text and words - Kent Gavin / Terry Nibbs

© Pictures - Mirrorpix

© Cover Picture - Mike Lawn

© Design - Mpress (media) Ltd

LANCASHIRE COUNTY LIBRARY	
3011812557278 8	
Askews & Holts	18-Jan-2013
778.92 GAV	£30.00

Standard Edition ISBN number: 978-0-9572559-0-6

Limited Edition ISBN number: 978-0-9572559-1-3

MIKE FISHER
ORGANISATION
★ ★ ★ ★ ★ ★ ★

Designed and published by m!press (Media) LTD.

Unit Four, Ashton Gate, Harold Hill, Romford, RM3 8UF

For Gloria, Stephanie
and Tracy.

Acknowledgements

Acknowledgements

I have really enjoyed working on this book, it has brought back many memories, both joyous and sad. I wish my dear friend and colleague James Whitaker were here to see it, as we worked together on many of the assignments that produced these images.

Firstly I must thank the entire Royal Family for all their help and co-operation over the years, for without them this publication would never have taken place. I would like to think that Diana would have enjoyed this book too, as I hope her boys do.

Thank you to my Daily Mirror Editors over the years, Lee Howard, Tony Miles, Mike Malloy, Richard Stott, Piers Morgan, and Richard Wallace, and of course the Picture Editors, Simon Clyne, Alex Winberg, Len Greener, Ron Morgans and Ian Down.

To Inspector Ken Wharfe, Royal Protection Officer, who became a good friend.

Special thanks to Fergus McKenna, David Scripps, Manjit Sandhu, Vito Inglese, Rebecca McCarthy and all at Mirrorpix.

Lastly, but not least, Terry Nibbs for stringing these words together from my notes and our conversations, and of course a big thank you too for Mike Fisher and all at the Mike Fisher Organisation.

Contents

Contents

Foreword

Foreword

Kent Gavin is a pre-eminent British photo-journalist whose iconic images have featured consistently on newspaper and magazine covers throughout the world. A wealth of personal and intimate stories and anecdotes has filled his career with a colour and magic few of his contemporaries could imagine. Through his key position as Chief Photographer with the *Daily Mirror*, Kent had the privilege to become accepted as one of the few trusted and respected royal photographers. It is for this he is best known.

The intimacy afforded him by the Royal Family over the years ensured Kent was able to capture moments in history that simply were not available to other photojournalists, and certainly not the paparazzi.

The trust and respect reflected positively on Kent and often throughout his career he was able to capture the emotions and colour of the Royal Family's most intimate moments.

Kent was particularly proud of his relationship with the Princess of Wales, who, because of a mutual respect, often gave him photo opportunities unavailable to anyone else. One example graphically demonstrates the privilege afforded him. While Kent was on holiday in Marbella he was called by the *Mirror* Picture Editor and informed that Diana had chosen him to take the official photographs at Prince William's christening. His award-winning shots speak for themselves, something he will be eternally grateful for.

It is because of his respect and genuine affection for the Royal Family that Kent chose to remain anonymous and not breach royal protocol, but he is well known for being positive and forthright – if not a little cheeky sometimes – when he sees the opportunity for an image that might otherwise be lost.

One such photograph was obtained when Kent gave the Prince of Wales his very own special award...

See gnome photo inset:

'Prince Charles' sense of humour is legendary; he is a great fan of the Goons, and often withstood a torrent of banter from Spike Milligan with true bravado!' Kent recalls: 'I thought it would be a good idea to present the Prince with a very special award for his 50th birthday, one that encapsulated his humour and was also a cheeky sign of our respect for him.

ST.JAMES'S PALACE

17th December 1998

Dear Mr. Javier,

    I just wanted you to know how pleased and surprised I was to receive such an unexpected gnome from you all in Sheffield the other day. I was very touched that you should have thought of me in this way (!) and if you would like to see where your small colleague is lurking in my garden, you are very welcome to come on a visit next summer...

Yours most sincerely

'The Prince was addressing a Prince's Trust gathering, something very close to his heart, when he realised we had something up our sleeve!

'He accepted the award with great pleasure but then surprised us all by announcing that he would hide it in the garden at Highgrove, to where we would be invited at a later date for a game of hide-and-seek to find the gnome and have some tea!

'True to his word, a few weeks later we were duly invited and a great time was had by all. I must admit I was moved by the way Prince Charles treated us. It was his idea; this was not a formal shoot or photo-call but something he did for us, taking personal time from his hectic schedule. Thank you, Sir!'

As a trusted member of the inner enclave of royal photojournalists, Kent has witnessed first-hand some historic events, and was able to record them in his own inimitable way. He has built up a fascinating chronicle of royal experiences. From war zones to 10 Downing Street to the White House, and from superlative sporting images to Hollywood film sets, his experience now spans an incredible six decades.

In this time Kent has won virtually every major prize in the industry; included in his 131 awards are World Press News Feature Photographer, Press Photographer of the Year (three times) and Features Photographer of the Year, to name but a few.

Kent achieved Royal Photographer of the Year an unprecedented seven times, and Royal Photographer of the Decade twice, in the 1980s and 1990s, with many of his famous photographs of the Princess of Wales securing these awards.

Kent is justifiably proud of a one-off award created just for him. On the 25th anniversary of the Ilford Films Photographers Award in 1992, they created an award that has only been dedicated to Kent – News Photographer of the Age. The one and only.

His iconic images are instantly recognisable the world over, and few of his fellow photojournalists are fortunate enough to share in the respect and admiration afforded Kent.

The following images and anecdotes are testament to the dedication and pride in what has been – and still is – the driving force of his career.

Chapter One

Her Majesty The Queen

In a manner of speaking, Her Majesty Queen Elizabeth II was responsible for me getting my big break as a national newspaper photographer. I did not have royal patronage, but had the Queen not agreed to visit Ethiopia and the Sudan in 1965 I would probably still be hustling as a general-purpose agency cameraman.

I was employed by Keystone Press Agency at the time, and this was my first major assignment abroad. A test of character indeed, and as such I was determined to wring every ounce of kudos from it.

A spectacular coup from me could be my passport to the dizzy heights of photojournalism, something to which I strongly aspired. I had been pestering the *Daily Mirror's* picture editor Simon Clyne for some time, in my customary modest fashion, by letting Clyne know in no uncertain terms that I could single-handedly make the world's greatest newspaper even greater! My arrogant prose dropped on his desk and was enthusiastically ignored.

I would have to try something different. There's an old saying, 'The proof of the pudding is in the eating'. I jetted off to Ethiopia amid the giant and anonymous press corps that always follows Her Majesty wherever she goes.

Just how would I get a chance to witness those special moments when there's a fleeting chance to capture something truly iconic? I needed some luck!

Photographer Freddie Reed was the *Daily Mirror's* royal powerhouse, and smart and tough to go with it. Freddie was impossible to upstage, and no one could read a situation like him, so I had a daunting task ahead. But a few days into the tour Freddie was taken ill with gallstones; such was his standing that the Queen's own doctor attended to him, and promptly ordered him home on the first

available flight for the medical care unavailable out there!

I was fortunate to gets some great shots, and because poor Freddie was out of the picture (ouch), a series of my images of the Queen graced the hallowed pages of the *Daily Mirror.*

Kent Gavin was on the move.

Freddie Reed recovered fully and a few days later I was summoned by Simon Clyne to the *Mirror* offices at Holborn Circus.

I will always be grateful to Her Majesty for embarking on that particular tour. 'Thank you, Ma'am!

The following images are testament to this.

Here Her Majesty receives flowers from well-wishers after watching Aborigine dancers, who were certainly entertaining if not a little saucy! But clearly the magic of monarchy is still very real in Australia.

Her Majesty wrapped up snug and warm at the Royal Windsor Horse Show, one of her favourite events. She enjoys playing host to her friends in what has become a standout event in the royal calendar!

The Royal Family love an afternoon of polo at Smith's Lawn, Windsor, especially when Prince Charles was playing. Here he is kissing his mother's hand after his team won the match!

Still on the 2000 tour, here she is visiting the War Memorial in Canberra, where she laid a wreath as a sign of respect for the fallen.

The Queen's love of Australia is undoubted, and at the opening ceremony of her tour in Sydney she gave a wonderful and heart-warming speech, finishing on the subject of the Republic of Australia referendum. To tumultuous applause she stated, "I have always made it clear that the future of the monarchy in Australia is an issue for you, the Australian people, and you alone to decide by democratic and constitutional means. It should not be otherwise. As I said at the time, I respect and accept the outcome of the referendum."

She went on to assure them that it was her duty and pleasure to serve and remain true to Australia's interests as we entered the 21st century.

This memorable shot of the Queen was taken at the British Legion Field of Remembrance at St Margaret's, Westminster Abbey. The moving occasion was made even more poignant by the fact that it was the Queen Mother who usually attended this event, but she had died eight months earlier.

I could see that the Queen was trying hard to control her emotions, and I felt for her; she was visibly moved and I pondered whether I should use the shot as it may have been seen as disrespectful at such a private moment. But it shows her honesty and warmth, and the grief of losing her dear mother.

This is a rare shot of the Queen, the Duke of Edinburgh and Prince Charles with the Duchess of Windsor. A real piece of history: if it weren't for Wallis Simpson's controversial marriage to the Queen's uncle, the former King Edward VIII, and his abdication, Elizabeth II would not have come to the throne until his death in 1972.

A lovely shot of Queen Elizabeth the Queen Mother, with her daughters Elizabeth and Margaret, Prince Edward (standing behind his mother), the Duke of Edinburgh and Edward's lovely wife Sophie, the Countess of Wessex, on the balcony at Buckingham Palace.

The Queen looks marvellous here, and this is another of my favourite shots of her. I keep saying that, don't I?

Her Majesty found particular joy on a state visit to Bangladesh in November 1983, where there had recently been plenty of publicity about the plight of children there. She was delighted to witness the excellent work being carried out at the Save the Children Centre in Dhaka. She is pictured holding a baby's hand, accompanied by the Medical Director, Dr Sultana Khoum, and other dignitaries.

The publicity Her Majesty got during the visit raised awareness worldwide and saw an upsurge in aid for the children.

Somehow Her Majesty always seemed to understand the shots I was out for and whenever possible did her best to accommodate. I was really up against it during her tour of the United States in 1976, the bicentennial year. When President Gerald Ford was hosting a dinner in her honour, a dance was also scheduled and a shot of Her Majesty dancing with the President would be like gold dust.

Getting into position at the right time would be almost impossible. The White House press department has a reputation for being highly sophisticated and super-efficient, but it certainly wasn't working for me! I mentioned to Ronald Allison, the Queen's Press Secretary at the time, that the big impact snap would be them dancing. Ron said he would see if this could be arranged, and it was, to the best of his intentions, but with the White House press people in charge it was not going according to plan!

Their photographer of course had access to everything and I was out in the cold!

Dancing would take place after the cabaret, and a song by the Captain and Tennille was the cue. Waiting, seemingly imprisoned in the press room, imagine my horror to see on a television monitor the Queen already dancing with the President.

The White House had let us down! What's more, I had only minutes to capture the shot or I would miss the deadline for the morning papers.

Leaving the press room without permission was strictly forbidden, but I thought 'What the hell!' and ran. By the time I reached the ballroom the dance was coming to an end; even worse, the two couples (Prince Philip was partnering the First Lady), were on the far side of the vast room.

Her Majesty glanced in my direction, and seemingly recognised the anguish and horror in my expression. With nothing more than serene but positive guidance she deftly turned the President around and brought him within range. Minutes later this shot was on its way to London. Now that's what I call co-operation!

This shot needs little explanation. Another opportunity for Her Majesty to attend the Derby, and here she is clearly delighted with the outcome of the race, accompanied in the royal box by Prince and Princess Michael of Kent.

A one-off visit to Britain by Pope John Paul II saw him as a guest at Buckingham Palace for a private meeting with the Queen. While the pair chatted away happily as he was leaving we were able to (unhurriedly for a change) get some great shots of His Holiness that appeared on the front pages of the next day's newspapers.

This was to celebrate the Queen's 60th birthday. Delegations from various schools were in attendance to see Her Majesty on a walkabout in front of Buckingham Palace, and there was what seemed like an endless line of children with daffodils, all waiting patiently to give them to her. I remember much giggling and squeaking going on, especially from the girls, and the Queen disappointed none of them, the photo-call ending with her arms full of flowers. A real hard-working mum.

A colourful turnout for Trooping the Colour. The Battle of Britain wing – Lancasters, Hurricanes and Spitfires – were flying over the Palace as I took this shot so as to be sure of getting some reaction.

This was a great day out for all of us, although security surrounding the American head of state was intense, to say the least! President Reagan was light-hearted and genuinely keen to ride with Her Majesty through the Home Park at Windsor. We weren't allowed to get too close (their security, not ours) and of course we would have loved some shots of them at full gallop since both were excellent horsemen. Ronald Reagan's experience as a Hollywood cowboy stood him in good stead, and they both enjoyed the moments of freedom away from us without getting too competitive.

On her way to open Parliament in November 1981. The state coach pictured here is used only for certain occasions and the Queen enjoys her journeys in this traditional royal manner.

A lovely family shot, and as I mentioned earlier, taken at the Princess of Wales's personal invitation. The christening of Prince William really was one of the highlights of my career; not only did I win a coveted award but also I spent one of my most enjoyable days at work ever. I love it when a plan comes together.

We had a lot of fun on this day, everything was going smoothly, there were no delays and everyone was in a good mood. The Queen was to unveil the Canadian War Memorial in Green Park, directly opposite Buckingham Palace, and the Princess of Wales was there too. A nice local job, it was interesting waiting to see what Diana was going to wear, as she always looked great, and had a natural understanding of what to wear and how to wear it. But sometimes she did surprise us! On their arrival the Queen and Diana were amused to see they were both wearing the same colour, a royal fashion faux pas. A coincidence or was someone being a bit naughty?

The Queen with a definite Asian flavour at a gala performance of Andrew Lloyd Webber's Bombay Dreams in London's West End. The event was in aid of the Commonwealth Institute and the Red Cross, of which she is patron. A great evening was had by all, and me in particular. What a show!

I know I seem to be saying this too often, but this is one of my very favourite shots of the Royal Family, especially as I was able to share some very intimate moments on what was a great day filled with humour and fun. In this particular image everyone is enjoying the Braemar Highland Games, and the Queen has just handed Geoff Capes an award for caber tossing and shot putting. (Poor Geoff is just out of shot in this pic. Sorry, Geoff!)

The Queen shook his hand, which much to her surprise was covered in a waxy substance to help his grip. Everyone laughed when they were stuck together, briefly, but fortunately she had gloves on!

One of my favourite pictures of Her Majesty taken at Bourke on her 2000 Australian tour. It was her 13th official visit to Australia and I know that she has a very special place in her heart for those 'Down Under'. I believe she enjoyed that tour immensely; there had been some negative publicity surrounding the Royal Family at that time but the welcome that she got from the people of Australia was truly overwhelming, as the genuine joy on her walkabout shows.

The Queen looking great in a diamond and ruby tiara and necklace. Fabulous jewellery is an integral part of the monarch's image. Her personal jewellery is quite distinct from the Crown Jewels at the Tower of London. Much of her collection has been presented to her as gifts or has been inherited. She owns some of the world's finest, most historic, pieces.

The Queen's love of horses and horseracing is legendary. A genuine form of recreation, she looks forward to days out at Epsom or Ascot, while a win by one of her horses is the icing on the cake. Here she is with her racing manager, the Earl of Carnarvon, animatedly willing a horse on!

The investiture of Charles, Prince of Wales, during which he spoke in both English and Welsh. This was a particularly memorable shot for two reasons: I was in a bad spot for what I wanted, and when I got the shot it won me an award! I had to get it framed just right with the battlements of Caernarfon Castle in the background, and the Yeoman of the Guard just in shot in the foreground, to make a great composition.

The next thing I needed, and the most important, was for Her Majesty and Prince Charles to notice and acknowledge me. The picture says it all!

Happy families! There was enormous hype and heaps of public affection for the marriage of Princess Anne to Captain Mark Phillips in November 1973. Everyone wished them well and we all hoped that they would both find lasting happiness. This moment of hilarity came about when the Queen noticed a banner in the crowd directed at the horse-mad couple: **"IT'S TOO LATE TO SAY NEIGH!"**

This image of the Queen pausing in thought among the headstones of the fallen in Normandy was my idea. The problem was getting her away from Prince Philip so I could get the shot I needed. I explained this to the Foreign Office guys and the Queen's Press Secretary and they said they would see what they could do.

Two minutes later Prince Philip left the Queen alone briefly and the shot graced the front page of the *Daily Mirror* on Tuesday June 7th 1994. Thanks again, Your Royal Highness.

Shortly after, a contingent of soldiers and veterans performed a march-past in front of Her Majesty, and then in a moving speech she observed: "Many of you will have in your minds vivid pictures – some perhaps all too vivid – of that epic day, and of the heroism and endurance shown by our own troops and by our allies. Those of us who were far away can only imagine what it was like. It was you and your comrades and our allies fighting on other fronts who delivered Europe from the yoke of organised barbarism from which the men and women of following generations have been mercifully free."

Chapter Two

Lady Diana Spencer, Princess of Wales

The dramatic life of Diana, Princess of Wales was enacted against a backdrop of interesting foreign destinations and genuine friendship with many world leaders. These are inextricably linked to some of the most significant events in recent history. Who can forget the lonely Princess at the Taj Mahal, the "War of the Waleses" in South Korea, the glamorous Diana, darling of the Manhattan fundraisers, or the "Queen of Hearts" in an African refugee camp or the minefields of Angola? These are just some of my recollections and iconic images I captured while travelling with her.

My personal relationship with Diana was that of a very close and trusted ally. In fact it was my first encounter with her that was to change my life forever.

It had been widely reported that Prince Charles was seeking a bride and there was talk of several women in the frame. The *Daily Mirror* had discovered that a young woman was being linked with Charles, potentially as a future Princess of Wales. That young woman proved to be Lady Diana Spencer.

I was able to take some endearing early photographs of Diana, and before long there seemed to be a mutual respect developing as I would not intrude or force any potential photo opportunities.

I soon realised that this beautiful, shy and innocent girl was very special indeed.

A natural rapport developed, and I was appointed royal photographer; although I didn't realise it at that time, my life had changed forever, and we were destined to become true friends – as much as is possible under the circumstances.

Her inner strength and determination to do her duty as she saw it shone all the more heroically because – as she was usually quick to admit – she was not perfect. But she was dedicated, and in all her years as a royal "tourist", Diana never drew a word of criticism from her hosts. She never committed any diplomatic blunders.

'*The Will to Win*'.

Princess Diana looking beautiful and straight from the hairdressers on her way to work. "Do you like my new haircut, Gavvers?" "Oh yes, Ma'am." It was front-page news the next day.

The Engagement of Prince Charles, the Prince of Wales to Lady Diana Spencer. On the banks of the River Dee at Balmoral.

A lovely spring afternoon at a care home in Bethnal Green, where Diana was warm and affectionate towards the elderly residents. The lady being gently stroked by the Princess was moved to tears by the interest that was shown. It was a pleasant and unhurried engagement.

Visits to Russia often bring something original to the mix, and make a refreshing change! This was certainly no exception as this engagement at a maternity hospital in Moscow shows. Mothers are being educated in the mechanics of baby care. And I mean everything, from the cleaning of little nooks and crannies to the perfect application of a disposable nappy!

A great day out for us all here; Diana was in fine form and made the most of the opportunity to have some fun. The Official Secrets Act forbids me from giving too much away but one thing that stands out in my mind is Diana's comment as I got this shot: "Watch out, lady driver!"

On an official trip to Canada, Diana and Charles visited an area of historic interest. It was suggested that she wore period costume for the occasion and she was only too happy to oblige. Not only that: she enjoyed the day and was really beginning to master her royal duties. Everyone was delighted and I got this great shot that highlights her natural innocence and eagerness to please.

Although their paths didn't cross often, Princess Anne and the Princess of Wales got on well together and respected the fact that they worked in completely different ways; Diana being a little more outgoing and tactile while Anne was the consummate if somewhat reserved professional. This was an early shot of them together, taken at Smith's Lawn, Windsor, on 27 July 1981, two days before Diana married Anne's brother.

Sorry to sound selfish, but this was another wonderful time for me. Sometimes I found it impossible to distinguish whether I was on holiday or at work and this trip to the Caribbean was most welcome after the mad rush of the previous weeks. My colleague James Whitaker and I were covering a skiing trip in Klosters when we got the nod that Diana was planning a Caribbean holiday with her Mum, Frances Shand-Kydd, and the boys. James and I left Klosters still wearing our skiing attire and caught a flight to Antigua.

We were in Business Class to make sure we were with the Princess and her party. But the plan went wrong. Diana, William and Harry were in Economy (very sensible) and we looked a bit daft! I managed to smuggle myself into Economy, where I was spotted immediately by a beaming Diana, "I don't think you're going to need your ski clothes where we're going, Gavvers!" she said.

Diana really enjoyed meeting Pope John Paul II, and particularly liked the outfit designed especially for her for the encounter. She was fast becoming a great ambassador for the United Kingdom by this time, but when meeting the Pope I detected a hint of the early shyness that endeared her to the world. They chatted away happily and although I'd photographed the Pope before, he had always been very reserved. I had never seen him so animated and having so much fun as when he was talking to Diana.

Children suffering the world over for whatever reason were one of the Princess of Wales's main concerns, and the work she did for children's causes was always dedicated and professional. Here she is spending quality time with the children of the "Hearts of Britain" campaign and is cupping the head of one child to console her. Diana also posed with the other children in the group.

This was very sad shot for me, Diana sitting alone at the Taj Mahal. I remembered what Prince Charles had said on my previous visit there with him. He stated that he would bring his bride there one day and be photographed on the bench with her. A portent of things to come, perhaps. Charles was in Delhi while we were here.

The VJ-Day 50th anniversary parade on The Mall in London, August 1995. Princes William and Harry were there with their parents and the rest of the Royal Family, but the boys were the stars of the show that day.

A simple shot of Diana in Bahrain. As luck would have it the light was perfect for me here, bright sunshine throwing enough reflection into the shaded area to give a perfect tone to her face. The wooden structure of the well doubled as a perfect sectional frame as she helped the women with the flowers.

The official visit to South Korea in 1992 was a big thing for me at the time because of the political power struggle that was going on in the region, coupled with the fact that this was my first visit there. Sometimes it is prudent that a little extra security is around when the heir to the British throne and his wife are visiting areas of unrest. This was one of those occasions, and in addition to royal protection officers we also had members of the Parachute Regiment! Diana enjoyed some flirtatious banter with them, as this series of shots illustrates.

A gala event during the Australian tour saw Diana looking absolutely fabulous in this full-length blue dress. She glanced over just after I got this shot and gave me a lovely smile. I should have got that shot too but I'd lowered my camera and was smiling back!

One of my favourite shots. "It's raining"! What more can I say?

Diana was never one to shirk a challenge, and in this case her visit to the minefields of Angola was an opportunity to highlight the plight of the people in the affected areas and bring to the world's attention the horror wrought by countless landmines sown indiscriminately in both open countryside and on roads in heavily-populated areas.

This was something close to her heart, and she was determined to do what she could to help. On her first walk down the minefield I didn't quite get the shot I wanted, and asked her to do it again. It was a long way! They had assured us that the mines had been cleared from the area, but how sure can you be? It was a lot to ask. She looked at me with those big blue eyes, smiled, and did it again. What a girl!

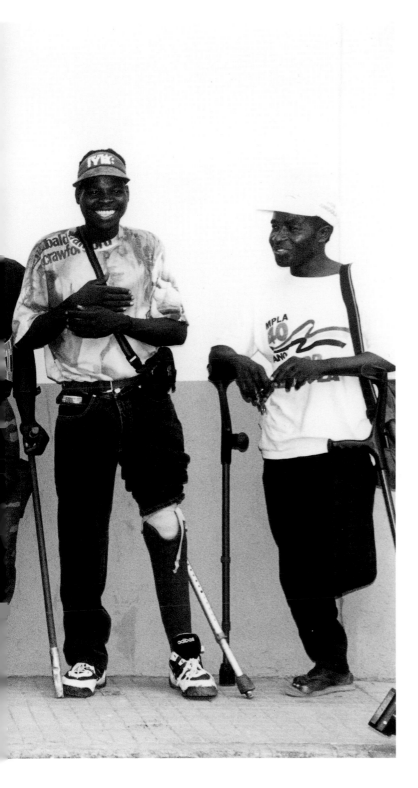

Another perfect example of royal co-operation. On an official visit to Luxor we had the chance to be tourists as well as workers and I got some great shots, but I really wanted one of Diana with the Pyramids in the background. She thought this a little cheesy and politely declined, but with the help of her protection officer, Ken Wharfe, I explained, "Ma'am, the Pyramids are one of the Seven Wonders of the World, and, Ma'am, so are you!" She looked at me, giggled, and with a twinkle in her eye replied, "I can't refuse that, can I?"

While there we also visited the tomb of Tutankhamun. In the tomb itself there is not much room at all, just enough for a couple of people to view the sarcophagus, so only one photographer could go down with the Princess to get a shot. I was the lucky guy and so a guide took me down to wait for Diana. When I got down there it was dark, the only light coming via reflections from up top, but no flash was allowed. Forty-five minutes later I was still down there waiting, a little apprehensive and sweating, when she arrived with the guide. "Spooky! Are you on your own, Kent?" "I am, apart from Toot, Ma'am."

Royal Ascot is always high on everybody's list for a good day out, and although the crowds sometimes make it difficult to get the right shots they also offer the opportunity to play "Spot the Royal" in shots like this. Diana was as keen on horseracing as the rest of the Royal Family – and most of us photojournalists!

Diana with Princess Grace of Monaco at Goldsmiths' Hall in the City of London, March 1981. This was Lady Diana Spencer's first official royal outing after she and the Prince of Wales got engaged, and we already loved her. Both women were destined to perish as a result of car crashes.

This is one of the most memorable photographs I have ever taken, but for all the wrong reasons. Here the emotions associated with such an awful occasion are so graphically displayed. I did not look for recognition or co-operation here; in fact I remember avoiding eye contact with any of the Royal Family. Prince Charles' concern for his sons is all too apparent, while Earl Spencer's expression is a mixture of anger and grief.

When news of the accident in Paris broke, my friend Piers Morgan, Editor of the *Daily Mirror*,

phoned me and told me that Diana had been involved in a car crash and was seriously injured. My heart sank and I watched in horror as the story unfolded on TV. On my way to the office it was announced that she had passed away.

I was in shock, in a daze actually, very emotional, and could not help shedding tears. I could not believe it was true. Taking this photo of Prince Charles and his two sons at Diana's funeral was without doubt my worst day at work. What a terrible waste of a wonderful young life was my overriding thought.

Chapter Three

The Royal Children

The Queen and Prince Philip are fortunate to have four intelligent children, all fascinating characters in their own right, which makes life far more interesting for one of the great observers of our time. I have always very much enjoyed photographing the Royal Family, and got a special kick out of some of my snaps of the children – and eventually their own children – and capturing images with historic value. The Royals vary in character, attitude and temperament, and their children are no exception.

Whether at home, on duty or at play, the British royal children have been a wonderful source of interest for an increasingly inquisitive world, and have continued to live colourful lives in the public eye. The royal ranks are growing ever quicker, the Queen and Prince Philip now have two great-grandchildren, and the desire for images and information about the royal offspring shows no sign of abating. The ever-hungry media circus will always be looking for great stories and photographs.

The first sighting of a new prince. Charles, Diana and their new arrival leave St Mary's Hospital, Paddington. A wonderful introduction to the world as the infant Prince William gets his first glimpse of daylight and the media throng that he will attract for the rest of his life. No one could foresee the tortuous journey ahead for the innocent new addition to the Royal Family, a child destined to be King and one who has developed into a fantastic ambassador for his family, Great Britain and the Commonwealth.

Prince Charles was in fine form on his visit to this historic settlement at Calgary on the Canadian tour. He was always a little suspicious when asked to don costume, expecting that we would look for a humorous slant for the following day's newspapers. This day was no exception but he was only too happy to oblige. It did backfire on us a little as he wore the costume with pride, and much to the delight of the native Indians present fulfilled his duty with respect and dignity.

Princes Charles and William at the VJ-Day 50th-anniversary commemorations in The Mall, August 1995.

Princess Anne had agreed to do a rare exclusive interview on the understanding that we would not ask questions other than those relating to her work with the Save the Children Fund. We agreed. My colleague Anton Antonovich was the Daily Mirror's top feature writer and I explained to him that on the recent tour of Africa the Princess did some great stuff but did not pick up any babies in front of my camera, robbing me of the high-impact shots I wanted.

I asked him to slip in the question "why not?" during the interview, hopefully without her twigging it, and he did. Princess Anne went quiet, gave me a 'Gotcha!' look and said to Anton, "He told you to ask me that question, didn't he? I do the job my way!" There was no doubt in my mind that Anne was referring to my tours with Diana, who found it natural to pick up babies.

The privilege often afforded me by the Royal Family over the years ensured I was on the spot to get shots normally unavailable to anyone else. This series of pictures from Prince William's Christening, at the personal invitation of the Princess of Wales, have featured regularly in this publication as it was one of those situations where I was able to take my time and get the shots I really wanted. In fact it was directly after this one that I made the suggestion regarding the Queen Mother holding the Prince that got me the famous prize winning image of Queen Mum smiling broadly as she held the infant William.

This really was a great day at Balmoral: Charles and the boys on the banks of the River Dee on 12th August 1997. Days like that really made my job an absolute pleasure, and it is clear that they too are enjoying the beautiful surroundings in one of their favourite places. My photos, because of the subject matter and the need for close and intimate images, often fail to show in detail the absolute beauty in this part of the world. It is no wonder that Balmoral is so popular with the Royal Family. No one had any idea of the tragedy that would befall the Princes just two weeks later.

Prince William shares his mother's understanding and tolerance of our need to do our jobs – provided we don't overstep the mark! I have always done my best to get on with the job in hand with the least possible intrusion, and usually achieved this with the co-operation of the Royals, for which I am ever grateful. On this occasion Prince William found himself in Glasgow on a Prince's Trust sortie and we were delighted to see dancing girls – always good for a fun shot – and this was no exception. William was a great sport, as the images testify.

Diana and Harry on his way to Mrs Mynors Nursery School in Notting Hill. This was a big step for a royal child, especially one who is third in line to the throne, to attend such a school. The Princess of Wales underlining her desire for 'normality' raised a few eyebrows.

The arrival of a royal baby is always the hottest and most joyous news, but the press was kept some distance away, making a good shot difficult. I was particularly lucky to catch this moment as Diana admires little Prince Harry when leaving St Mary's Hospital, Paddington, with Prince Charles.

A typical family group shot, taken when Charles and Diana were guests of King Juan Carlos and Queen Sofia of Spain on Majorca. The two families have a mutual admiration and respect; true friendship is rare among royal dynasties but absolutely genuine in this case.

William's first day at Wetherby School in Notting Hill. Diana left Kensington Palace telling William that it was important to behave well in front of the photographers outside the school. "I don't like 'tographers,'" William interjected loudly, a phrase that became familiar to those close to him throughout his childhood. During the journey, under police escort, Diana laughed with him telling him, how smart he looked in his bright new uniform, but at the same time taking the Mickey!

The Princess, however, explained that this was the beginning of royal life, and despite his dislike of "tographers" he would out of necessity have to get on with it, since the media would play an important role in his life.

The police had corralled the huge bank of assembled media and upon his arrival at the school William waved to the "tographers" as instructed. A polite handshake with the headmistress Frederica Blair-Turner and William rushed inside to meet his new classmates. The parents of the other new boys, dressed in their finery, smiled at William and his mother, hoping for a chance meeting and a long-term friendship with royalty.

Polite conversations ensued, until one small boy was ushered in William's direction, having been given a positive steer by his mother. He came to a halt, close to William's face, and in a shaky voice asked, "Is it true you know the Queen?" To which William replied, with a calm voice, "Don't you mean Granny?" Diana laughed loudly with her instantly recognisable screech! The ice had been broken.

"Prince Charles misses William's first day at school!"

On the eve of William's first day at school I went to see Phantom of the Opera at the Haymarket Theatre in London, and was having a pre-show beer in the bar when Graham Smith, Diana's protection officer, approached me. I commented on the fact that musicals weren't his cup of tea and he laughed. "Where are you sitting, Kent?" he asked. "Let me see your tickets."

"Is Diana here?" I enquired, and he laughed again. We finished our drinks and took our seats. Just before the curtain went up Diana walked in and sat in front of me! We chatted for a few minutes and she asked if I was going to be there in the morning for William's first day at school. I confirmed that I would be.

"My husband is going to miss it; he's snowed in at Sandringham." Eureka! "Excuse me, Ma'am, I have to make a phone call..." The curtain went up as I was on the phone to the *Mirror.*

'World Exclusive' front page: "Prince Charles misses William's first day at school". That is what you call privileged information. I can't imagine they were seated exactly in front of me by coincidence. Thank you, Ma'am and Graham.

In my humble opinion Princess Anne is the hardest working of the Royals, making time for the many causes she believes in. The good thing about Anne is you know exactly where you stand with her! She is not one to mince her words, and you soon discover exactly what you may or may not do.

I know she really enjoyed this trip to Zimbabwe as President of the Save the Children Fund, which she has been since 1970. Her joy was obvious by the manner in which she reacted to the children and doctors at the orphanage. The whole trip was a great success, and another paid holiday for me. To this day I still can't believe my luck being paid to do something I feel so passionate about, and it was great to see Victoria Falls again. Princess Anne seemed impressed too.

Klosters has long been known as a royal playground, and our Royal Family have done their best to uphold this tradition. This really is a favourite, especially among the young Royals, who are all accomplished skiers and can't wait to get on the piste! Princess Anne's daughter Zara joins uncle Charles and her two cousins for an action-packed adventure.

This is one of a sequence of shots taken on Charles and Diana's tour of New Zealand. It was particularly memorable because this was the occasion of the infant Prince William's first crawl on camera. Diana particularly enjoyed this, being immensely proud of her son.

Here he is in Auckland standing with help from Mum and Dad and wobbling in front of us, when all of a sudden there was an exodus as we packed up our cameras to make ourselves scarce.

This did not escape Diana's notice and she later asked why we didn't make the most of this great moment. I explained that New Zealand was 12 hours ahead of the UK and to catch that day's newspaper deadline we had just minutes to spare. We made it!

Great shots these. Prince Harry and chums during a breather in the Eton Wall Game. Played on St Andrew's Day, the tradition dates back to the building of the curved brick wall alongside the Furrow at Eton College in 1717. The pitch is just five metres wide and 110 metres long; many a grazed knee and bloody nose have occurred in its history! Harry thoroughly enjoys the rough and tumble of this competitive tradition – and competitive he most definitely is.

A sad gathering at Windsor Castle. Princess Margaret, the Queen's sister, is laid to rest. Margaret was a fascinating character, who because of royal protocol at the time was unable to find companionship with the man she loved.

Prince Harry's first day at school; following in his brother William's footsteps at Wetherby School was an absolute delight. Diana had always stressed to the boys that they should have as 'normal' a life as possible under the circumstances, and even at this tender age Harry was doing very well. The Prince by this time was noticeably artistic and sporty and had a real interest in anything military. According to Ingrid Seward's book William and Harry, he had a tough time adjusting to school at first but his happy-go-lucky attitude got him through it.

A Klosters theme is developing here. This is a familiar image of the three Princes that appeared in newspapers and magazines the world over, and is one of which I am particularly proud. It was a day of trouble-free tranquillity, and Charles and his two sons were as kind and co-operative as ever but, more importantly, their sense of fun made the day!

Diana, William and Harry at Niagara Falls on their Canadian visit. The boys really loved this day; in fact it was a great success for everyone. Here they have just boarded the famous 'Maid of the Mist' and on their return were soaking wet after an amazing voyage under the falls.

Prince William and Zara Phillips, now Mrs Zara Tindall MBE, 14th in the line of succession, and BBC Sports Personality of the Year 2006 share a private moment. Like William, Zara yearned for a 'normal life' and she has achieved this. A great girl.

Sarah, Duchess of York with daughters Beatrice and Eugenie at Verbier again. Andrew was at work, and unable to be with them on this break.

The first day at 'big school' was a trial for me, I remember, but Prince William appeared calm and relaxed from the start. He was escorted to Eton College by Mum, Dad and brother Harry, and welcomed by his housemaster, Dr Andrew Gailey. Although Charles and Diana had separated by this point they continued to support their children together.

*Following in big brother **William's** footsteps Harry had tea with **Dr Gailey** and his wife **Shauna** before donning his uniform. Here he is on his way to his first lesson.*

Another pleasant afternoon's work, this time in the Waleses' garden at Kensington Palace. Diana looked fantastic and Charles was relaxed and in good humour. I remember this day particularly because it was long before William's "I don't like 'tographers" pronouncement and he was performing brilliantly for the cameras.

A day at Sandringham getting some fun shots of Prince William playing on a fire engine. The private setting of the royal Norfolk estate provided a welcome change from the hubbub of an open photo-call.

A hairy ride with Prince Andrew in a lift to the roof of a building adjacent to Ground Zero in New York. As we got into the lift, the operator announced that it hadn't been confirmed that the lift was 'safe' after the 9/11 attack. We exchanged anxious looks and held on. The view from up there was incredibly moving for both of us. A sombre experience indeed.

Prince William was in adventurous form when he joined the RAF Mountain Rescue Team on Holyhead Mountain in Anglesey, North Wales, to practice emergency life saving and rescue skills. He jumped at the chance of some tough rock climbing and while he was there carried out all aspects of the rescue operations which he would be called upon after his training.

Chapter Four

Royal Holidays, Official Visits and Tours

Royal tours, wherever or whenever they take place, are a hectic time for us photojournalists to say the least. The feeding frenzy that is a holiday, visit or tour, taxes everyone's patience to the limit. Striving to get the right shot, or be in the right position to at least have the chance of one, is our aim. It is at these times more than ever that I have often been fortunate, or even blessed, to receive co-operation from members of the Royal Family that certainly surpasses their duty towards the media.

Apart from being a little cheeky sometimes, and expressing my opinion if I really believe that we are likely to miss a great shot, I have made a conscious effort to be there to do my job but in no way intrude on their privacy. I have never asked for a photo to be taken with any member of the Royal Family, or tried to 'muscle in' on sensitive moments like some of my media colleagues.

Whenever I have been pictured with Royals, it is always at a dinner or award ceremony where I was a recipient or party to the news itself, and not in my role as photojournalist. But sometimes in the chaos of battling through the lines of my fellow photographers I am grateful for every little bit of help I get. And I am proud to say that Her Majesty has given me that help on a number of occasions.

Colonel Frank Borman story

It's no secret that I have photographed all the members of the Royal Family on many occasions, and along the way, especially on the holidays, visits and tours, that I have become the Queen's greatest fan. I know how tired I get when trailing her on royal outings, so I can imagine how exhausted she must become – an average day's work for the Queen on tour would shatter anybody. But she rarely shows it and her good humour and patience are quite remarkable. Having said that, and meant it, I must admit

there was one time when I saw her get a little testy, and that was with her husband.

Prince Edward, who was five at the time, was due to receive a gift from astronaut Colonel Frank Borman at Buckingham Palace. Borman was Commander of the Apollo 8 space capsule that orbited the moon in 1968 ahead of the first lunar landing. Prince Edward was to receive a model of the capsule from the pilot himself, every child's dream!

The Queen wanted the model to be put aside and presented later; Prince Philip and yours truly wanted it done then so I could get the shot. Seeing the pair squabble over something so trivial was amazing, but a little embarrassing. They were human! I tried not to listen, but being right next to them it was impossible not to overhear without sticking my fingers in my ears. They were no different to any other couple. By the time Colonel Borman was escorted into the next room the matter had been settled. The Duke of Edinburgh and I had lost!

Her Majesty on a tour of Bangladesh. Here she is pictured visiting an orphanage in Dhaka. She was visibly moved by what she witnessed and the tour proved to be a great success for me as well as the Royals. I was getting the hang of this 'Royal Photographer' thing, but to be honest at this stage I was still wondering what I'd done to get the best job in the world. I have never taken my good fortune for granted.

Charles and Diana with the boys on board King Juan Carlos of Spain's yacht. They were on holiday as guests of the King and his family on Majorca. The two Royal Families have a long-standing relationship, and I know that Charles and Diana made the most of the privacy afforded them.

I made this hat myself to a trusted Australian recipe, and carried it for two weeks with me on the royal tour, just waiting for the right moment to present it to Prince Charles and get an atmospheric shot. He gave me a funny look (I was at it again) and asked, "Does it really work, Mr Gavin?" "I don't know, Sir; the Aussies wear them though!" He put it on and we got some great shots. Fair Dinkum, sport!

Prince Charles' meeting with Indira Gandhi was a formal affair, with political machinations going on in the background. This particular shot was memorable though because the light gave the photograph a mysterious quality, an effect that sometimes you just get lucky with.

St Tropez again and this shot appeared in newspapers and magazines all over the world. Diana had a great time with her boys on this holiday, and jumping into the sea made for a great image.

This is one of the most reproduced pictures I have taken. The private holiday in the Caribbean was greatly anticipated and Diana was really looking forward to it. A private holiday with no photo-calls. To cut a long story short, my colleague James Whitaker and I negotiated the possibility of a sort of unofficial opportunity with Ken Wharfe, Diana's personal protection officer, with whom I had become good friends, for a shoot to take place. After some deliberation and several meetings we had something in place. But we had to let other journalists in on it, and do exactly as Ken said as we were breaking all sorts of security protocols.

In addition there had to be a three-day news blackout – no images allowed to escape prematurely! The photo-call took place, us aboard locally hired boats, and Diana appeared with the two boys on cue. Thank you, Ken. We all got our shots, but I got the magic one! I kept in touch with Ken for the three days after and surprisingly everyone did as agreed. No leaks, and I got the best shot of all.

This was an official visit to Hungary; we had just arrived at the airport and were aware that as part of the official greeting the royal couple would inspect a guard of honour. The Prime Minister and his wife were to join them, but the Prime Minister's wife was feeling nervous, shaking in fact at the thought of this very public appearance. Diana took her aside and comforted her as only she could, and then took her by the hand and led her through the inspection. Diana told me the whole story at a reception later. What an ambassador!

African tours were always great fun, as traditionally there would be native topless dancing at some stage, which Charles always took in his stride, although he did look a little uncomfortable sometimes. Here Prince Harry accompanies his Dad, the trip coming soon after Diana's death, and he seems to be coping very well.

Here we are, back in New Zealand and this time it's Charles who gets the official greeting. Tours "Down Under" are always popular with the Royal Family as between engagements they have a chance to get away from it all in spectacular settings. Australia and New Zealand have a very special place in the hearts of the Royals.

Princess Anne on an official visit to Zimbabwe, pictured here with a young patient, his doctors and nurses, and the hoard of officials always in attendance at these events. Anne is not so tactile as Diana was, but her concern for the causes she embraces is genuine. But you have to be on your best behaviour with Anne, as she is very dedicated and professional. If you don't act in the appropriate manner or overstep the mark you will most definitely know about it. I am pleased to say I managed that over the years and enjoyed working with her.

Ascot again, and a right royal day at the races. Another opportunity to play 'Spot the Royals!" Who can you see in this shot?

This was one of Diana's favourite photographs. We were at the Pavarotti concert in Hyde Park and it was raining cats and dogs. That didn't stop everybody having a great time, and the show was brilliant. Pavarotti was a wonder and he and Diana enjoyed some great after-show banter. When she saw this photo she requested a copy for herself. Was I chuffed or what?

Another outstanding day in the life of a royal photographer. Just setting foot on the world's largest nuclear-powered aircraft carrier is indescribable, but I'll try. It is absolutely huge – a floating city – but the Duke and Duchess of York took it in their stride and did not seem as awestruck as I was. They lapped up every minute of their visit and Andrew was given the opportunity to take what must be the greatest rollercoaster ride on the planet by rocketing off the bow in a jet fighter.

Verbier again! An eventful day on the piste. The Duchess of York always made the most of these breaks, especially if her dear friend Diana was around. It's clear that Sarah and her daughters Eugenie and Beatrice are having a great time on their Ski-Doo!

Private holidays are without doubt what Princess Diana loved best, especially when she was able to be the 'Fun Mum' that she was and play with her boys. Here in St Tropez she is jumping in for a dip while Harry, fast becoming a confident adventurer, decides to stay on the jet ski and have more fun.

Another opportunity on an African tour for Charles to witness first-hand the delights available to royal personages!

A great shot of Charles and Diana flirting at the races.

This really was one of the milestones in my career. Apart from football, and being a genuine fan of the Royal Family, international politics has always intrigued me; I have been fortunate to meet many of the world's leaders and witness the machinations of their lofty positions.

White House security has always been incredibly tight on any occasion that I have experienced, whether at home or in the USA.

When I found out that I was going to be in the same room as Russian President Vladimir Putin and his wife Lyudmila I was over the moon but expected security to be tight, to say the least, and they were actually staying at Buckingham Palace as guests of the Queen!

Their arrival was quiet and dignified and Lyudmila looked fabulous. Not since 1874, when Tsar Alexander II came to London following the marriage of his daughter, Grand Duchess Marie Alexandrovna, to Queen Victoria's second son, Prince Alfred, Duke of Edinburgh, had a Russian leader been a house guest of the Queen.

Security of course was tight, but not overwhelmingly so, and the mood was intimate and light-hearted. It was a real privilege to be in the presence of such dignitaries at a truly historic event.

Her Majesty enjoys playing host to visiting dignitaries, but on this occasion the presence of President Clinton and his wife Hillary for lunch at Buckingham Palace was much less formal than usual. Certainly less so than other visitors to the Palace had experienced. There were plenty of American Secret Servicemen around but the President was confident and jovial, without a hint of embarrassment after the recent Monica Lewinsky scandal.

There's nothing the Queen loves more than a day at the races. When she went with her mother you knew there was going to be fireworks, and if they had a winner then all the more to celebrate. Here they are sharing some tips and observations with the Earl of Carnarvon again, the Queen's racing manager.

Wildlife and nature's wonders were two of Diana's favourite subjects, and she was truly delighted to witness a whale up close and personal off the coast of Puerto Piramide during an official visit to Argentina.

This was Princess Diana's first visit to New Zealand. On our arrival in Auckland there was a formal reception, and as usual the Maori officials were keen to maintain their traditional welcome for dignitaries to their country. You have to rub noses. Diana was happy to uphold all that is dear to the native representatives, to the delight of everyone present, including Prince Charles – who had already been through this a number of times. A great shot was created.

Agnes Gonxha Bojaxhiu, Nobel Prize winner, human dynamo, better known as Mother Teresa of Calcutta, pictured here with Prince Charles on his visit to Calcutta. What a woman. To quote her: "If we have no peace, it is because we have forgotten that we belong to each other."

Prince Charles is always a good sport, and after a brief welcome to the medieval mass football match the teams hoisted him aloft and you could see that he was a little uncomfortable. "Don't drop me!"

This 800-year-old sporting tradition is close to the hearts of the people of Derbyshire. It was Charles' job to start what is recognised as the 'maddest' game of football on the planet. Hoisted aloft by players to 'turn up' the ball, the official way to start, he was carried by three players in Ashbourne for the ancient Shrovetide football game. He then addressed the thousands of spectators who had gathered for the official opening ceremony, saying, "Long may this fine Derbyshire tradition continue, in this great country of ours. I only hope that someone scores a goal!" He then threw the hand-stitched leather ball into a throng of several hundred combatants.

The game is played over two days on a three-mile course by the 'Up'Ards' and the 'Down'Ards', decided by whether you were born north or south of the brook that runs through the town. The rules are few and far between, most notably 'manslaughter is not considered good sport' and 'motor vehicles are not permitted.' Horse and carts are!

This photo-call was great fun, with Prince Charles enjoying spontaneous banter with the Spice Girls in the presence of Nelson Mandela. Mr Mandela was in fine form and openly flirted with the girls, which greatly amused Charles. Geri Halliwell was her usual ebullient self and definitely game for a laugh. It was a magical moment when she asked Mr Mandela how old he was, and on his reticence to answer her immediately, snuggled up to him and squeaked the immortal line, "You're only as old as the woman you feel!"

Another enjoyable break for Princess Diana in Lech, Austria, on a sleigh ride with her two favourite men. At play with her precious boys saw Diana at her happiest, and the three would always be getting up to something – and often quite happy to play up for the cameras. It is these moments that made my job an absolute pleasure and privilege.

Two Kings on the up at Klosters.

*"**WHHEEEEEEEEE**" Prince Charles and Harry enjoying some son-and-dad time on the slopes at Klosters.*

A rare visit for the Queen and Prince Philip to Romford Market in Essex. Her Majesty was overwhelmed by the welcome, and her walkabout provided some great banter with the stallholders and was often hilarious. The 'Del Boy' aspect of her subjects was certainly not lost on her.

Chapter Five

Prince Charles

I must start this chapter by saying that all through the story of Charles and Diana I was able to remain neutral, as my affection and admiration was evenly balanced between the two. From the word go it would always be difficult for them juggling the royal balls to maintain the equilibrium. Charles' relationship with his mother and father had always been strong, and he had been taught to be polite and respectful to all he encountered as a member of the Royal Family and heir to the throne.

Like his sister, Princess Anne, Charles is a hard worker, and although not quite so robust in his nature as Anne – due to, I believe, his great sense of humour and fun – he is always efficient and professional with the task in hand. I would like to think that Charles' attitude towards me over the years is one bordering on real friendship, as he often gives me help and attention that I have not witnessed with others of my ilk. For that I am most grateful, because, without the help and co-operation of your photographic subjects, the really great images remain elusive.

The marriage of the Prince of Wales to Lady Diana Spencer. What an event! What a story, this really was the biggest royal occasion in decades, and I was lucky to be in a position to get the honeymoon shot of them on Britannia. The "Look of Love" was a prizewinner for me, and we thought it would be a good idea if we could follow the couple on their yacht. So we hired a boat, at a cost of £20,000 I recall, to tail them in the Mediterranean and get more shots. Well, it was a great time for all of us: there was

plenty of beer, wine and good food about so we made the most of it!

We never saw them once, not even a glimpse of their yacht, and found out later the skipper of our boat was a good friend of their captain. No wonder, we were on a hiding to nothing! But we had a great time. On our return from our voyage we were invited to Balmoral and I took this photo on the banks of the River Dee. All's well that ends well.

Many happy returns, Chuck! Prince Charles receives a birthday surprise with Robbie Williams and ex-Spice Girl Geri Halliwell.

Smith's Lawn, Windsor, again for the après-polo presentations for the Cartier Polo Cup, one of the highlights of the season. Charles is receiving congratulations from an old friend, actress Susan George, in a hospitality marquee.

Seeing the topless torso of this 'patient' at an Australian paramedic centre, Charles looked at me and said: "I know what you're up to!" Although he didn't attempt the chest compressions he did demonstrate mouth-to-mouth resuscitation.

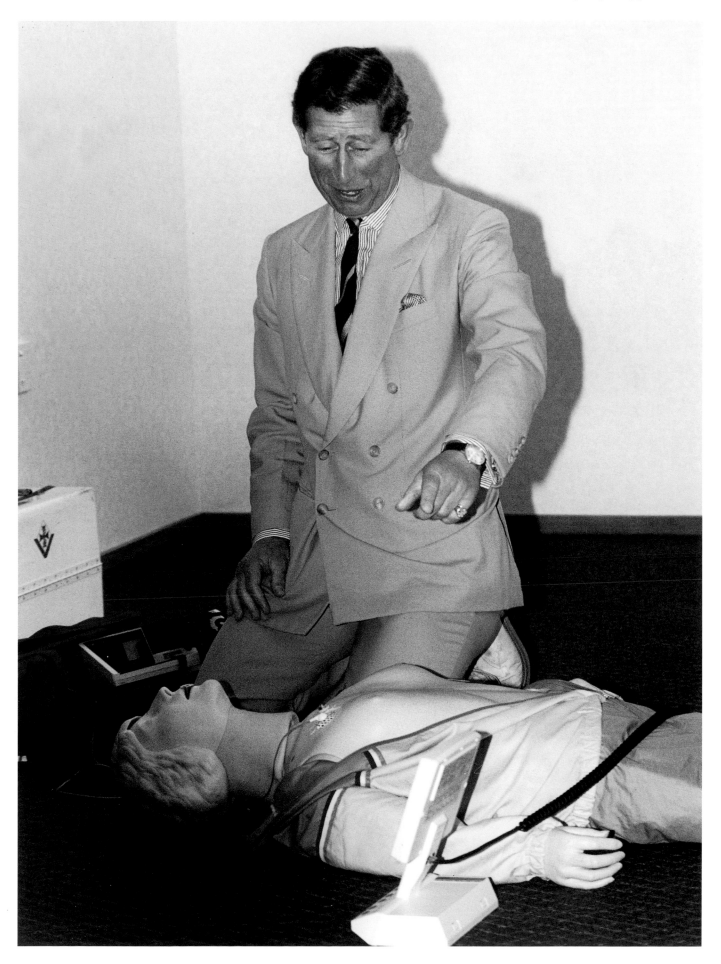

Few people realise that Charles, like his sons, really is an action man, and incredibly fit. If you've ever tried windsurfing you'll know what I mean. On this trip to Australia, his power swimming through heavy surf made some great shots, but when he got on the windsurfer he was strong and accomplished. I never knew he'd been on a windsurfer, but having tried it myself I realise just how strong you must be to get back on after a mishap. Getting up speed and maintaining it is especially difficult and takes ages to master. He flew along, much to the delight of those present, and I got this award-winning shot.

The proud father at the christening of his first son, Prince William. As I have mentioned before, I was personally selected by the Princess of Wales to take this series of shots. Diana is comforting the baby by letting him suck on her finger, providing a brief respite from his tears.

Prince Charles' face says it all as he takes another opportunity to enjoy the local talent, one of the dancing girls at this official engagement in Buenos Aires on the Argentinian tour.

A beautiful day, an even more beautiful location. Royal Deeside, in which Balmoral Castle is situated, is a well-established favourite of the Royals, and here Princes Charles and William are making the most of their time and getting back to nature.

As I have mentioned earlier, Prince Charles always does his utmost to comply with my wishes where possible. But he is always on the look out for a mischievous set-up. This series of shots shows him entertaining some schoolchildren by trying his hand at golf – not a bad swing; cricket – looks quite at home at the crease; and baseball –very comfortable here too! The kids had a good time and so did Charles, apart from his bad back giving him a nasty twinge on the golf swing.

Smith's Lawn again and after a strenuous game of polo it's time to get a prize from the Queen. Charles, the dutiful son, kisses her hand in thanks. It's hard to say who enjoys these day the most.

Onwards and upwards. The wedding of Prince Charles to Camilla Parker Bowles took place in a civil ceremony at Windsor Guildhall on 9 April 2005. This event was a long time in the making. Charles had known Camilla for more than 30 years and it was common knowledge that they had been very close friends, often linked romantically. Now the Prince of Wales and the Duchess of Cornwall can enjoy their freedom and I wish them all the best.

Rastafari! On the Caribbean tour we were being entertained exuberantly at Trenchtown Community Centre in Kingston, Jamaica, and during the fun someone handed me this hat with a Rasta wig attached, Too good an opportunity to let pass, I handed it to Prince Charles, who examined it carefully, gave me a knowing grin and put it on back to front quite deliberately. Brilliant.

As part of his Royal Duties Prince Charles always made the most of meeting with the workers from all fields, and was quite happy to get his hands dirty sharing their experiences. On his visit to Australia he made the most of his visit to a mine where he engaged in some great banter with the miners and everyone had an enjoyable and relaxed day.

That must have hurt! Charles and his mount part company at a polo match in Windsor. These incidents are not uncommon for the Prince or his sons and fortunately there was not much damage done on this occasion. Their competitive nature and sheer enjoyment of the sport is testament to their upbringing; you have to expect a few knocks now and again. Charles' attitude remains positive at times like this and such occurrences are endured in relatively good spirits.

Charles and Camilla in their carriage at the Sandringham Flower Show. They are looking relaxed and comfortable at what is always considered by the Royals to be a good day out.

Just a few feet from the edge of a very long drop, Prince Charles enjoys an afternoon at Kaieteur Falls on his trip to Guyana.

The reason I chose this photograph of Prince Charles on an earlier visit to the Taj Mahal to open the chapter is because it was taken at a time of great expectations within the Royal Family and the unfortunate incidents in the recent past were seemingly over. The Taj Mahal is regarded as one of the most romantic places on earth, and it was well reported that Charles was on the look out for a bride. He often made jokes on the subject, much to our delight. After the photo had been taken, Charles light-heartedly confided, "I'll bring my new bride back here one day, Mr Gavin."

Prince William spent a month working on The Duchy Home Farm as a farm labourer as part of his gap year. The main part of his project was organic farming, but William really got into the swing of things and did just about everything that a farm labourer would do. He worked hard with a great attitude, and thoroughly enjoyed his time there.

This was one of my favourite shots for a long time. The investiture of Prince Charles on 1 July 1969 was a big day for both of us, and I got an award-winning shot! There wasn't much time to get the action pic I wanted as the landau passed, and even though I was getting more royal co-operation than I could have wished for, this was one of those situations where the carriage was just going to pass and the occupants – the Queen, Prince Philip, Princess Anne and Prince Charles – had no idea I was there. They had quite enough on their minds, as you can see from the reaction they were getting from the crowd. A happy day for all concerned, despite the huge security issues.

The Prince and Princess of Wales cut a rug at Government House in Melbourne, Australia, in happier times. She is wearing a £2-million diamond and emerald choker. This is Sarah Ferguson's favourite picture of her dear friend.

I regret closing this chapter on what might seem a negative note, but this photograph bears witness to a sad period in our history. In South Korea, Charles and Diana had a hard time hiding the fact that their marriage was 'over'. It was the "War of the Waleses" time, a difficult period for both of them. The fun that they would once have had on such a visit was clearly absent.

I couldn't resist this shot of Charles animatedly testing the 'pull' of this bow at an archery and clay pigeon shoot demonstration on a Prince's Trust outing in Berkshire.

Chapter Six

The Queen and The Queen Mother

The British Royal Family has evolved enormously in the last one hundred years, and for over one hundred years of her own life, Queen Elizabeth the Queen Mother played a major role in the giant public-relations exercise that is royalty today. The Queen Mother devoted herself to her royal duties and won the hearts of the nation with her infectious enthusiasm and joy. A wonderful mother to her daughters, and the perfect grandmother, her relationship with her family was strong and full of love.

Her story is unlike that of any other royal; in fact as a member of the powerful Bowes-Lyon family, the owners of Glamis Castle, they were respected the world over. During the First World War, Glamis was opened for wounded officers to recuperate, much like in the TV series Downton Abbey. After their convalescence the young officers would write to the beautiful young Elizabeth Bowes-Lyon, and she always took time to reply.

Her father was powerful and opinionated, and not too impressed by the Royals of that time. Lady Elizabeth was introduced to the Royal Family by Princess Mary, the only daughter of King George V and Queen Mary, who met her through the Girl Guide movement of which both were members. Elizabeth ran the Forfar branch at Glamis and Princess Mary often visited for inspections and jamborees. They became firm friends.

Lady Strathmore encouraged the relationship. Elizabeth was one of ten children and her mother was keen to find her a good match, with Princess Mary's brothers being eminently suitable. Elizabeth was definitely ' Deb of the Day', loved and admired by many would-be suitors, including Prince Albert, 'Bertie', soon to be Duke of York.

With a dogged determination he pursued his quarry and after turning down Bertie's proposals of marriage three times, Elizabeth succumbed to his wonderful nature that by this time had become apparent, and won her heart. Romance had sought her out; she found the man she wanted to spend the rest of her life with and they married. Then, by a twist of fate that would be considered fanciful in a Barbara Cartland novel, she became Queen.

King George VI and Queen Elizabeth undertook their royal duties in the very best of tradition, endearing them to the nation even more. Their love of animals in general also started a fairly modern royal tradition. In 1933 they bought a corgi, 'Dookie', from a local breeder as a pet for the young Princesses Elizabeth and Margaret, and a family love affair with the breed was born, as this shot with her beloved corgi at Clarence House on her birthday many years later shows.

*The Queen and the Queen Mother looking fabulous
on the balcony at Buckingham Palace with the Prince
and Princess of Wales after Trooping the Colour.*

A helping hand from her No. 1 Grandson.

The smile says it all!

The Queen Mother pats her great-grandson Harry's back. An unusual shot, but it shows how tactile and affectionate she was to her beloved boys on her 89th birthday at Clarence House. The birth of Prince Charles delighted her and he became the son she never had; her love for all of her boys was no secret.

It was unusual to see this little group together, and I can't remember the reason for it. Everyone was enjoying some happy banter, and Princess Margaret was looking particularly well, but before too long ill health began to trouble her until her untimely and premature death in 2002.

The Queen Mother here with Prince Charles at the Garter ceremony. The Most Noble Order of the Garter is the oldest and highest British order of chivalry, founded in 1348 by Edward III. I remember this day so well as the Queen Mother had stepped up a gear and her exuberance was clear for all to see. The day will stand out in my mind forever. And another prize-winning shot in the bank!

Clarence House again for the 99th birthday photo-call. The Queen Mother, seen here with her children and grandchildren, looked fabulous as usual.

The Queen Mother's sense of style is apparent here, and her humour too, as Prince William's laugh shows. Sorry if I seem to be going on about this, but you will have noticed that I was the Queen Mother's biggest fan. She had a natural eye for fashion, and after being introduced to Norman Hartnell instantly fell in love with his use of cut and colour, creating the look for which she became famous.

Following the death of her mother, Lady Strathmore, just before an important state visit to France in 1938, Elizabeth went into mourning. Hartnell suggested she do so in white – definitely a break with royal tradition – and produced 30 outfits for her in just two weeks. She took Paris by storm – sadly before my time as a photographer – and singlehandedly repaired Anglo-French relations. "We have taken the Queen to our hearts,' newsreels reported at the time.

"She rules two nations; France is a monarchy again." This was big news, and was carried out with a style and verve that was quite simply her own.

Whenever the Queen Mother was seen in public she was usually smiling and had an infectious wit and charm that bewitched everyone. Always wearing floaty pastel shades, she was Norman Hartnell's biggest fan and his favourite client. A feel of the spring or summer was always around her, perfect for attending the flower shows she loved. Whenever I was fortunate enough to be near her she was extremely helpful. A real PR genius, tough as old boots too, and her sense of fun was an absolute delight.

The Queen is terrific. She understands what photographers want and is always tries to oblige, especially when travelling abroad. Likewise the Queen Mother, who was as popular with members of the press as she was with the public.

Very often there were no other photographers around, or perhaps my peers simply did not have my vision, as was the case with my award-winning photograph of Prince William's christening, when I captured a magic moment as the Queen Mother, William's great-grandmother, proudly cradled him in her arms.

The photo-shoot, attended by one TV crew, myself and only one other photographer, had drawn to a close.

I was surprised that no official picture of the Queen Mother and infant William had been requested, especially as it was her 82nd birthday, and so, in an act that some might consider a serious breach of protocol, I addressed the Queen personally and suggested the sitting take place.

Her Majesty agreed with my observation and was delighted to accommodate my wish. Another award-winning, iconic image was created.

A family gathering to celebrate the Queen Mother's 94th birthday at Clarence House. What a trooper!

Another Birthday Bash for the Queen Mother and she is clearly having fun on her meeting with these youngsters. She always adored being surrounded by children, and spent some time with them as they presented her with posies, bunches of flowers and a special balloon, which she particularly enjoyed. whole royal family for dinner and photo.

'The eyes have it': dedicated followers of the Derby!

*Trooping the Colour gives the nation a chance to see the **Royal Family** doing what they do best. The custom dates back to the time of **King Charles II** in the 17th century when the colours of a regiment were used for rallying the soldiers in battle. They were trooped daily in front of the men so that they would remember where their rallying point should be when raised and didn't fight alongside the wrong regiment! Simple but true. Here the **Royal Family** are watching a flypast, a much more recent addition, but always a great photo opportunity.*

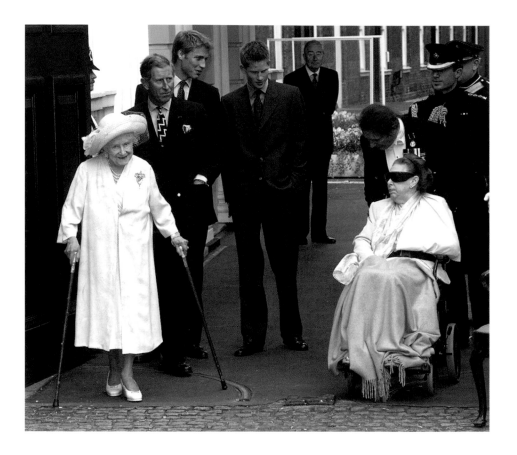

Queen Elizabeth the Queen Mother on her 101st birthday, her last. She still had the magic and energy that was her trademark, as this picture shows. Her beloved daughter Margaret is pictured here with her as the Princess's health continues to fail.

The term 'end of an era' is often used, and usually unjustified or exaggerated. In the case of Elizabeth Angela Marguerite Bowes-Lyon, daughter of the Earl and Countess of Strathmore, born on 4th August 1900 and who passed away at Royal Lodge, Windsor, on 30th March 2002, aged 101 years, seven months and 24 days, the term could not be more justified.

She was a royal giant who took the world by storm and left everyone she met smiling and infatuated with her.

Prince Charles and his two sons, Princes William and Harry at the Thanksgiving Service at St Pauls Cathedral. Charles is giving a helping hand to his grandmother, the Queen Mum as she is being greeted by the Dean.

I have always got on exceptionally well with Prince Andrew. He is an absolute gentleman and has made my life much easier on a number of occasions. He married Sarah Ferguson at Westminster Abbey in July 1986 after she arrived fashionably late in the Glass Coach with her father, Ronald Ferguson. The Queen had earlier made Andrew Duke of York, a title last held by her father, which is traditionally conferred on the sovereign's second son. A crowd of 100,000 people clamoured outside Buckingham Palace to witness the first public kiss of the newlywed Duke and Duchess of York.

Sadly Andrew's marriage to Sarah failed to stand the tests of time, partly because of the Duke's frequent absences due to his naval service, though they remain close friends and care equally for their two beautiful daughters, Beatrice and Eugenie.

The Queen Mother's 80th birthday celebration at Clarence House with the Queen and Princess Margaret, the corgis in the background.

One hundred not out! Her Majesty's 100th birthday is marked by an appearance on the balcony at Buckingham Palace with her daughters Elizabeth and Margaret. I don't know how she did it! This really was a milestone that many thought we wouldn't see. Well done, Ma'am.

Queen Elizabeth the Queen Mother and Prince William leave St. George's Chapel, Windsor. On my first royal appointment there it was pouring with rain and I arrived early; luckily the Dean invited me in for coffee and we chatted as I waited for the royal party to arrive.

During the conversation he became aware that I was interested in royal history and he told some fascinating facts about the table at which I was sitting with my coffee. I seem to remember having my elbow on the table at the time, and instantly removed it.

"The table on which your coffee is standing has one of the most macabre royal stories in history. It is the very piece of furniture on which Charles I's headless body was laid immediately after his execution at Whitehall Palace."

He also showed me the ledgers including drawings of the collapse of the floor, and the actual spot where Henry VIII's body had laid. Wow! A few weeks later I was at the Banqueting House in Whitehall and went up to the first floor and stood on the spot where Charles I had stepped out for the chop. Real history!

Chapter Seven

Kate and William

A Modern Romance and a very Royal Wedding

The marriage of Prince William to Kate Middleton has seen the end of centuries-old royal tradition. I think the Royal Family have come to the conclusion that perhaps the individual concerned should make up their own mind on their choice of spouse. Princess Elizabeth was fortunate to meet Prince Philip, and it was practically love at first sight. He ticked enough of the boxes to satisfy all concerned at the time, and the attraction between the two was genuine, not too common in royal circles unfortunately. The Queen witnessed her sister Margaret's failure to find happiness with divorcee Group Captain Peter Townsend, who unfortunately didn't fit in. Although in love, they were not permitted to marry.

Prince Charles' marriage to Diana Spencer promised much and had fairy-tale potential, but sadly things were not to work out, proving that royal suitors were few and far between. Fortunately for Charles he had a dear and longstanding friend in Camilla Parker Bowles to ensure romantic security after all he had been through. Future happiness for the Royals in this enlightened age could only work in one way: freedom.

William and Harry were open from a very early age with regards to their future wishes; they wanted to be as 'normal' as possible, despite the constraints they face. Their mother actively encouraged them to mix freely, show respect for others and live as normal a life as possible. I think they are doing a great job.

It is not unusual for a commoner to come to the attention of the Royals; history has certainly proved that. But now we have witnessed a significant development with William marrying his long-time girlfriend. Kate's background is certainly comfortable, her parents are successful business people, and she was already becoming a society 'princess' with the sound and privileged upbringing she had experienced.

Kate really can be all we wish for: she is beautiful, glamorous, quick-witted and has taken to royal duties like a duck to water. She and William are clearly in love and this is a wonderful opportunity for the Royal Family to move on from the ups and downs of recent times.

Prince William met Catherine Middleton in 2001 while studying at St Andrews University in Scotland. They were genuinely attracted to each other and before long a relationship had developed. When the story of their romance became public the media attention she got was sudden and torrential. And the camera just adores her. Speculation that they were going to marry became the most talked-about subject in the media and when they announced that were splitting up in 2007 it was bad news for us. Kate and her sister Pippa had become celebrities in their own right by this time and although she would always attract plenty of attention, royal stories without Kate just did not have the same appeal for most of us, especially me.

They continued to be close friends throughout the separation and the best news the media could wish for was granted later that year when they rekindled their relationship. The word was, and not just wishful thinking on our behalf, that it was back on – and serious. It was!

They announced their engagement on 16th November 2010. At last!

When Kate started to accompany William to high-profile royal events and engagements we knew that the wedding would not be far away and they married at Westminster Abbey on 29th April 2011. I am happy to share some of those moments from that day with you.

I know that Diana would have approved of Kate, and been so proud of William on his special day. He in turn would have wished his mother were there to share his joy; perhaps she was in spirit. I hope so.

Wills and Harry have arrived. For someone about to make the biggest commitment of his life, Prince William looks remarkably calm as he enters Westminster Abbey to marry Catherine Middleton. Their romance was actually quite conventional for that of a royal couple, and I hope they enjoy as much freedom and privacy as their hectic work schedule and royal commitments will allow. What a wonderful King and Queen they will make.

In the last few minutes as a single woman Kate looks like she is really enjoying the event. Pippa, seen here holding the train, is another beautiful girl and will hopefully benefit from being linked to the Royal Family in such a positive manner. Both girls are a credit to their parents, who have obviously brought them up extremely well. Pippa, a society star, has recently been linked to the Duke of Northumberland's heir, George Percy, after accompanying William and Kate on several skiing holidays. They claim to be just good friends but Earl Percy has been seeing a lot of Pippa, and it's not the first break they've shared with William and Kate.

Earl Percy, 27, has been seen with the Duke and Duchess of Cambridge and the Middletons on the slopes of Meribel, the popular French resort in the Alps. George and Pippa have known each other since they met at Edinburgh University and have also recently been seen skiing together near Geneva. The Old Etonian is heir to his father's estate that includes Alnwick Castle, 'Hogwarts' in the Harry Potter films. Could it be Duchess Pippa one day?

A wave to the crowd as Kate Middleton goes in with her father Michael, now on the look out for new staff for the Middletons' company Party Pieces to replace Kate as her royal role will prevent her from continuing to work in the family business. Kate's mother Carole set up the business in 1987 after finding it difficult to locate everything needed to successfully host a children's party. Twenty-five years later they have gone from strength to strength.

No sign of pre-wedding nerves as Kate enters Westminster Abbey. In another break with royal tradition she arrives by car from the Goring Hotel accompanied by her father Michael, but will be travelling back to Buckingham Palace in the 1902 State Landau. Interestingly, the Royal Family and the Middletons are paying for much of the wedding, so it won't be too much of a burden on the taxpayer! Very thoughtful.

They decided on Westminster Abbey as the venue for their wedding; they could have got married anywhere they liked, but chose it as it had hosted the weddings of the Queen and Queen Mother and sadly the funeral of William's mother.

William and Kate emerge from the abbey to a tumultuous reception. Married at last! The joy on their faces says it all as the newlywed Duke and Duchess of Cambridge leave Westminster Abbey enjoying the first moments of married life. The Dean of Westminster, the Very Reverend Dr John Hall, was delighted that they chose the abbey for their big day and said it was a very happy occasion for the couple themselves, for their families and friends, for the country and Commonwealth and for well-wishers worldwide. My sentiments entirely.

Andrew, Beatrice and Eugenie after the wedding. The girls looked fabulous, especially in their dramatic choice of millinery, though unfortunately their mother was unable to attend. It was reported that Prince William had invited Sarah some time before, though there was no evidence to confirm this. There were also reports at the time that international television companies and media giants had offered Sarah huge sums to commentate on the wedding, but that she declined them all. I think that was probably the right decision for Sarah.

More than a million people lined the streets of Westminster as the happy couple travelled in the 1902 State Landau, which was built by Hoopers for King Edward VII's Coronation. As they left for Buckingham Palace and the official reception the delighted crowds showed their appreciation and love for the couple as they drove past. There were around 1,000 invited guests at the reception from the 2,200 present at Westminster Abbey, which lasted until 3pm, when the royal couple were allowed a breather before a private party for some 250 guests – family and close friends – at 7pm. The celebrations culminated with the Duke and his new Duchess taking to the floor as man and wife for the first time. Congratulations!

As 2011 drew to a close I took these images of Kate and William and the rest of the Royal Family at Sandringham on Christmas Day. Kate is an absolute natural as a royal, and already has a great confidence and manner that endears her to all who meet her. I think she will carry on the most important royal tradition of all, the legacy left by the Queen Mother and Diana, Princess of Wales, and the example so perfectly set by the Queen, that of being kind, caring, full of fun and fulfilling her royal duties in her own way.

Sandringham at Christmas is a firm favourite of the Royals, and provides the chance for a break at the beautiful Norfolk royal retreat. Prince Philip was late on parade due to a health scare but was soon back on his feet and among his family again. There is no doubt that the recent marriage of William to Kate caused well-wishers at Sandringham to swell to record numbers, with a crowd in excess of 3,000 people outside the church to greet the Royals.

Kate looked fantastic and was the star of the day. Here she meets her new admirers confidently and professionally, and more importantly, gives her time freely to those she encounters on her walkabout.

Kate with Camilla and other members of the Royal Family, including her brother-in-law Prince Harry, the Duke of York and Princesses Beatrice and Eugenie.

Kate and William arrive at the Church of St Mary Magdalene as part of the large royal party.

These are just some of my favourite photographs among the thousands upon thousands of royal pictures that I have taken throughout my career. It was sad to leave a lot out, but there simply wasn't enough room to get them all in.

In this book I hope I have successfully shared some of my own personal royal moments with you. Now in my sixth decade of royal appointments, I have witnessed the happy, the sad, the downright hilarious, and the evolution of a very special family.

It has been a great honour for me and, looking back, has been more than I could ever have wished for. I'm a very lucky man, still enjoying what has been the driving force of my career for over 50 years. Once again, thank you, Ma'am, and your family.

KENT GAVIN frps